HIS DIRTY HANDS

NICOLE MERRITT

DEDICATION

THIS BOOK IS DEDICATED TO EVERY PERSON, MALE OR FEMALE, YOUNG OR OLD, WHO HAS HAD THEIR DREAMS SHATTERED BY A CALVIN, AND ROSE ABOVE THE HURT TO REGAIN YOUR IDENTITY AND MOVE ON IN LIFE. I DEDICATE THIS BOOK TO YOU FOR NEVER STRAYING AWAY FROM YOUR FAITH AND LETTING GOD LEAD YOU TO BUILDING A HAPPY, SUCCESSFUL, AND REWARDING LIFE. IT IS ALSO DEDICATED TO THE ONES WHO ARE NOW IN THIS SITUATION NOT TO BE INTIMIDATED TO TAKE THAT FIRST STEP. IT IS MY HOPE AND DREAM THIS BOOK MIGHT BE THAT FIRST STEP. FINALLY, I DEDICATE THIS BOOK TO YOU ALL WITH OUR LOVE, APPRECIATION, AND THANKS FOR ALLOWING ME TO BE APART OF YOUR LIFE.

CONTENTS

1
THURSDAY NIGHTS

Have you ever tried to make your life more complicated in the hopes that something more exciting might come around? A few years ago, that is precisely the kind of thing I would entertain. I thought that, perhaps if I made it to work a little later or a littler earlier, maybe I'd meet that special someone because I was willing to change things up a little and potentially land on a new radar. Mr. Right's radar would be more exciting than the calm and predictable lifestyle I had created for myself up until then.

Everyone was telling me how lucky I was to even have a job. The economy had tanked and just about everyone I knew was either out of a job or about to be.

HIS DIRTY HANDS

Friends who once teased me about my Management job at McDonalds were now wondering if we were still hiring. Of course we were and still ARE, hiring.

While I had grown accustomed to compliments about how responsible I was, it was one of those situations that left me restless. A single mother to two teenage boys, I was beginning to wonder what might be waiting for me beyond my role of motherhood.

Convinced that there could be more to my life than what was promised by the golden arches, it made sense at the time to consider every encounter, no matter how coincidental, as a welcome sign pointing to an even brighter destiny that was in store for me.

It was a soppy Thursday afternoon with hours still ahead of me. I hated Thursdays. Especially Thursdays like this one. The movie theater adjacent to this particular McDonalds would be showing the latest Batman movie tonight and our store was sure to be mobbed with rowdy teenagers either out with their friends or customers out on first dates.

It had been ages since I had even been out on a date and it was starting to concern me. On Thursday afternoons like this one, I was starting to wonder if my fear of becoming like my mom was in some way factoring into this now lonely Thursday night equation.

My mom was a sweetheart by even the highest standard. She was the type of woman who would do anything for her man and back in the day, that was all that mattered. In my mom's mind, her worth was measured by how much of a beating she could take at the hands of my father. Somehow, loyalty to my dad trumped anything she might have wanted to do with her own life.

Traditional values were important to her and while I questioned what was so "traditional" about nightly scenes between her and my father that mimicked any episode of COPS, I valued the lessons she taught me about forgiveness.

Now a parent myself, my boys actually know and have a relationship with their father. I can thank my mom for encouraging that trait in me. In a culture where too many boys don't know their dads, I prided myself on the fact that my boys did.

Not every relationship is meant to be, as I had painfully learned so many years ago when I separated from their dad. Back in the day, women like me were frowned on and considered over-the-top in our attempts at securing equality.

After too many fights and months of separation, we were able to put our differences aside and recognize that a happy life was owed not only to us, but to our children. Over the years, we would develop a polite and considerate relationship that would stand the test of time. Today, we can laugh at how I was too much woman for him and how I was suffering less headaches and frustration.

Now, years since our separation, no one of any brilliance had announced themselves to me yet. "Maybe I am being too critical?" I thought. Loneliness has a way of creeping into your every thought at times like these rainy Thursdays, when the rest of the world seems to be spinning happily along without you.

On this particular Thursday, I wondered if it was time to put my fears aside and allow a man to surprise me for a change.

Not every man is going to be as bad as my father was and with as many men as there are in the world, maybe I had not placed enough gambles.

The loud alarm signaling the next batch of fries jolted me out of my moment of reflection. Noelle was a new hire who just wasn't working out. She was either deaf or too dumb to care about the fries that would be ruined if the alarm went off more than once.

I had just been promoted and it was quickly becoming clear that if I wanted things done right, I'd have to do it myself.

Rushing to the greasy cages dripping with oil, Noelle nervously fumbled with the French fry sleeves while I instructed her on the proper way to scoop the fries. "Life HAS to get better than this," I promised myself.

Noelle was one of four new employees, within a month, who were on the verge of being replaced. It was a miracle I wasn't getting more complaints, but my hustle and drive to succeed would always be my saving grace.

Most of the high-school trainees were hired on a temporary basis. Few, if any of them, considered a job at McDonalds a real career choice. A few even seemed to take pride in failing at the most basic tasks. One of my few rewards was the feeling of accomplishment I felt about outshining just about everyone at work.

This Thursday afternoon was no different as Noelle in her nervous jumble, dropped the entire pile of French fry sleeves on the greasy floor.
Scrambling to pick them up, I was forced to take over at the drive-thru window as a shiny black Dodge Charger made its way up in front of me.

Trying desperately to disguise my disgust at Noelle, I managed a half-hearted smile in the customer's direction. I could tell instantly this wasn't just any customer as his calm but demanding eyes commanded my full attention.

His window only half-way rolled down, a handsomely groomed gentleman looked perfectly matched with his vehicle. "This guy is smooth," I thought as I had to remind myself I was at work and at the drive-thru window of all things. Managers didn't have to work the window as waves of embarrassment rushed over me.

"Why do I have to meet this guy HERE and NOW?" "Sounds like you have your hands full in there," he chuckled... and continued, "or NOT full." I was stunned that he had witnessed what had just happened with Noelle dropping the sleeves.

"I hope one of THOSE isn't going to be MINE." he went on in a deliberate tone that was careful not to sound too intimidating. "Oh don't worry sir, I'm the Manager here and I will make sure that one of THOSE isn't YOURS or ANYONE ELSE'S FOR THAT MATTER." Liking my come-back, he muttered, "well, okay then, but how do I know for sure?"

Meanwhile, a filthy work van full of construction workers had nestled itself a little too close for comfort behind the gentleman's pristine Charger, forcing "Mr. Smooth" to make an early exit muttering,

"Don't worry, I'll be back – D E M E T R I A."

Referring to me by name, he seemed to deliberate on every letter. Like a brand new pair of shiny shoes, he handled each letter with care. Dramatically repeating my name, "Demetria," this guy had a sophistication of a man who wasn't from this part of Georgia as he seamlessly handed me a twenty dollar bill telling me to, "just keep the change. I'll be back later."

There was something mysterious to the glint in this gentleman's eyes that assured me that he would be back. For some reason or another I hoped he would. It wasn't everyday a man with some standards showed up at my doorstep, or in this case window.

Of course, I was wearing the ugly plastic name tag that everyone was forced to wear as part of our uniform. Perhaps he could look past all of that and come back to finish the story he seemed so eager to start. I would have a response to his question, "how do I know for sure..." "Because, I'm in charge" would be my answer, and hopefully, he would like it.

2
MR. SMOOTH

I could barely understand Noelle as she tried to rehash what had happened only moments after I left for my one and only break that evening. It wasn't at all common for any of the trainees to call my cell phone, as most customer "incidents" were resolved with a free meal voucher and rarely required any Management involvement at all.

With the crashing of register drawers and through the loud cracking and smacking of Noelle's bubble gum, she was miraculously able to communicate most of what she needed to.

"Um, he asked for you by name and he pronounced it right," Noelle recounted, rushing through a list of "concerns" that he needed to discuss with "D E M E T R I A."

Remembering how he had pronounced my name, I couldn't help but get excited about the thought that the sophisticated gentleman from earlier this afternoon wanted more than just a conversation about new laws regarding health code violations. My store had stellar reviews and no one could argue the strict standards my management style had produced in the short time I had been there.

"So did you get his number and did you tell him that I would call him back?" I asked. While only minorly irritated that my break was being interrupted, I was more excited about the fact I would have a way to continue a conversation with him in private. Noelle responded, "Uh, no because he won't leave. I told him that you were on break and he said he would be fine just waiting for you."

"What!" I muttered under my breath in disbelief. I couldn't believe how tenacious this Mr. Smooth was being and wondered how a conversation would pan out in front of the entire restaurant. Noelle went on, "he's sitting in a booth in the corner by "The Playground" and was really nice about wanting to wait. He didn't seem mad or anything.

He just said that there are some things he needed to talk about with you in person. Oh! And, he also asked if you had a boyfriend. I hope you're not mad that I said no!"

I could just see Noelle expecting brownie points for her attempt to set me up on a date with this Mr. Smooth. It seemed she was desperate to hold onto whatever leverage she could to keep her job. While clumsy on the floor, she had a way with the customers that gave her an advantage over some of the other new hires.

But like so many young ladies her age, her dedication to following the rules was oftentimes erratic as her call to me during my break was risky and chomping on gum while at the register, even riskier.

Sitting on the damp step of the movie theater across the street, I watched the world stream in and out of my restaurant. Maybe I should be thanking Noelle for dropping those sleeves earlier instead of being in such a fix about it. If it weren't for her, Mr. Smooth wouldn't be impatiently awaiting my arrival. "Maybe this is the window of opportunity everyone keeps talking to me about," I thought.

Gathering my purse, badge and car keys, I snuck a peek at myself in the side-view mirror of my car.

Shockingly, Mother Nature was doing a decent job of taming what I thought for sure was the un-tamable. Being in "mom-mode" was becoming way too familiar. I was thankful for any help I could get in the dating department.

Looking into the mirror's slightly dented reflection; I was reminded of just how hard I had worked to make these wheels even possible.

Not as nice as Mr. Smooth's Dodge Charger, my Honda Passport picked up some serious slack when it came to the demands of two teenage boys. My mom had applauded my "responsible" choice while I benched the notion of buying a trendier car until the kids were out of the house. The navy blue family mobile seemed to wink at me as I brushed passed it, almost as if to say, "Don't forget about me in there!"

"How could I?" I thought. It had been hard enough raising two boys on my own much less being able to handle a car payment AND insurance. The economy had taken a toll on every facet of my life and the added car payment would be a critical component in securing my entire family's well-being.

I had found the now ten year-old car on Craigslist and spent the last of my savings to even get into the damned thing, there is no way I could simply "forget" the amount of sacrifice I had made on behalf of a lifestyle so many would consider barely getting by.

Catching a glimpse of the back seat, I fondly remembered when both of my boys were still in car seats. Not wanting to erase that happy memory, I would intentionally let animal crackers and Happy Meal toys take permanent residence under the sturdy plastic floor mats, not caring that the back seat would eventually become indecipherable from the front.

"Cluttered, like someone actually has a good life in here," my mom would say in response to my embarrassment about the mess.

"Life is messy," she would go on to remind me. "There is no such thing as a completely clean life." My mom loved the car because it saved her from the eight blocks she would have to walk in the hot Georgia sun in order to get groceries during the summer.

In comparison to the other cars in the parking lot that Thursday night, my car was merely an oily speck of sand on the most ordinary of beaches.

It had become invisible over the years because the boys would naturally evolve into young men themselves.

Both boys had cars of their own now. They no longer needed me to shuttle them back and forth from school or other activities. Mom was getting too old to enjoy going to the grocery store so trips with her were becoming fewer and far between.

The Passport's glory days now clearly over, the car's purpose in getting me to and from work seemed almost too practical, too predictable, too imprisoning. Opening the door to the McDonald's main seating area, I couldn't help but wonder what surprises might be in store with a man I knew only by the nickname, "Mr. Smooth."

Nowadays the 7:30pm dinner shift felt more like a high school gymnasium on game night than it did a restaurant. Teens and wanna-be hoodlums would hold the restaurant hostage for the rest of the evening while the movies across the street were either just starting or just getting out.

The play-area designed for preschoolers and toddlers would now operate as a lover's lane for those boys lucky enough to have more "game time" after movies with their dates.

Too often, the manager's role on nights like this one was to babysit its customers so as not to get the title of being one of "those" McDonalds. I would be damned if, after all of my hard work, my restaurant would get that kind of title because of a bunch of unruly teenagers.

Spotting Mr. Smooth in the back corner of the restaurant, we locked eyes in what felt like a romantic arm wrestling match.

My eyes telling him, "I know the REAL reason why you're here" and his eyes responding, "You THINK you KNOW, don't you?"

I politely nodded and motioned to my purse. I would need to put my things in the back in my storage locker prior to our conversation. Rolling his eyes in what seemed like an overly dramatic display of disappointment, Mr. Smooth was a mixture of over-the-top comedian and genuinely irritated.

I was intrigued that I didn't know which emotion reigned supreme for him and liked that on a night as predictable as this night had seemed destined to be, this sophisticated gentleman was keeping me on my toes.

In his immaculately starched and pressed olive suit, he stood out in stark contrast to the children at my store that night.

Mr. Smooth's dazzling eyes seemed to spit laser-guided sunshine darts in my direction as I ducked and weaved in between the young maniacs that were acting like they had just been released from a mental institution.

Telling one of the more convincing thugsters who was twice my size, that he needed to throw the pile of straws he had dumped on the floor away, I shoved my way past as he taunted me, "let me show you what I can do with it mommy." Ignoring his remark, I decided what waited for me in the booth would be far more entertaining than any go-round with a child. I already knew how that story would end and that wasn't something I wanted Mr. Smooth to witness, for the time being anyway.

"Best this 'Mr. Smooth' believe I can show some mercy," I thought and before I could even finish, Mr. Smooth had cleverly exited the booth and with both hands on the thugster's hoodie, said in the same deliberate tone he used on me earlier that afternoon, "Nah! Why don't you SHOW ME what to do with it M O M M I E?"

Shoving the kid back down and onto the end of a table, Mr. Smooth was a lot taller than I had imagined he would be. It was impossible to contain my grin but I managed, remembering my role as manager depended on my ability to maintain peace in my own restaurant.

"Sir" I barked, "PLEASE, it's alright! He was just kidding. That's what these thugs do."

Positioning myself in front of Mr. Smooth and the thugster, I turned my attention to the boy calmly asking him to leave the restaurant before he found himself in even more trouble. He obliged by unloading himself off the table and, in defiance, dropping yet another pile of straws on the floor on his way out.

Mr. Smooth, obviously irritated, dramatically bowed to the now audience of customers that had gathered to watch the scene. In a grand gesture reserved only for those meeting the Queen, Mr. Smooth stepped back from the narrow walkway behind a neighboring chair.

With hands and arms separated as widely as humanly possible, he proudly proclaimed, "since your Manager doesn't know what to do with the straws or the thugs, for that matter, why don't we let her take a BREAK... Mommies first."

Ushering me into the booth that once seemed like my window of opportunity, my heart was still racing at what had just happened.

Realizing my customers needed some reassurance, I half-heartedly told them to go back to their meals and that everything was just fine.

Not knowing whether I should be furious at this Mr. Smooth or grateful, it made more sense to quietly hear him out. I watched as he carefully wiped both of his hands with what looked like those disposable moist towelettes.

Noticing my curious gaze, he uttered, "These are for when I have to get my hands dirty. Thanks for that by the way." "Thank You for what?" I asked. I could no longer see his eyes, the eyes that had promised so much hope and excitement were now lowered onto his hands as he chuckled and nodded as if to say that I was just too stupid for not knowing what I should be thankful for.

"Dear, do you NOT understand that you should be thankful to men who have to get their hands dirty on your behalf?" Methodically wiping up and down the length of every finger, Mr. Smooth finished his hand washing routine and expertly folded the now parched towelette into what looked like an exquisite piece of origami.

"Here," I extended my hand over the table and nodded for the dirty towelette. I continued, "Let me take care of that for you." The tiny little piece of trash could just as well have been thrown off the Empire State Building. In the time it took to reach my hands, which seemed like an eternity, Mr. Smooth raised his eyes to lock with mine.

Again, in his deliberate tone he responded to my gesture, "THAT is more like it." The jolting rays of sun that had peeked behind the thugly clouds of that Thursday evening incident had now come out to play.

Mr. Smooth's large and perfectly manicured hands seemed to glisten in the artificial light of my McDonalds that evening. I thought, "This man knows how to take care of things. Maybe it's time to let someone take care of ME for a change."

While confused about what to make of his display with an unruly thug, I had to put myself in the shoes of a sophisticated man in an unsophisticated world. I doubted that Mr. Smooth was ever a regular patron of any fast-food restaurant.

Chance had dealt its hand that Thursday. Who was I to question what was clearly playing out? Perhaps it was time to listen to something besides the obnoxious demands of customers who didn't give one damn about my future.

"Can you hear that? It's gone off twice!" Mr. Smooth asked. The French fry alarm had made yet another noisy entrance into my already chaotic day. "Yessir, I do. That is precisely the reason we met earlier today and precisely the reason I must get back to my employees. Let me handle that and I can be back in five."

"Five?" he asked. This time he looked less infuriated as he sullenly mimicked a sad puppy, "oookay. I guess since you're doing your job, I can wait."

"K," I let my hand settle on his long enough to show him my positive intentions. Getting up and turning out of the booth, I caught Noelle out of the corner of my eye. She was so busy watching what was happening with me and Mr. Smooth, she had let a new batch of fries die in a vat of grease, a vat of grease that could have given me ten more minutes with a man who had just wanted to save my day. Instead, I would have to postpone my fairytale for a few more minutes.

After reprimanding Noelle for her lack of attention and for the oversized wad of gum in her mouth, I noticed Mr. Smooth was no longer sitting at the booth. A moist towelette had taken his place. Waiting for me at the now grimy table, the unopened package seemed to smile at me. In meticulous handwriting, Mr. Smooth had written his phone number in red ink, "CALL ME! Calvin."

3
WARNING SIGNS

"Calvin." I remember saying his name over and over, excited about his persistence and take-charge attitude in those early days of courtship. Everything about the man seemed to indicate that he was someone who had things under control. Even his voicemail seemed to be scripted to the syllable.

"Hello, you have reached Calvin Jones of Jones Enterprises and I am currently busy with another client. Please leave your name, number and a brief reason for your call and either I or my assistant will call you back expeditiously."

It impressed me that he used the word "expeditiously," a word that most people would have to look up.

As for the non-existent "assistant," Calvin was convinced that saying he had an assistant made him a more credible business man.

A lie that should have concerned me actually pleased me back in the days when an escape from a monotonous lifestyle mattered more to me than the truth of the matter. Jones Enterprises would become just as insignificant as his real job, baggage claim supervisor at Delta Airlines. Calvin was a master at fooling people, but I wouldn't figure that out until he had done a supreme job at fooling me first.

Just like any single mom, I did what I could with regard to doing my due diligence and asked all of the questions any female would ask about who Calvin was as a person. Claiming that he was new to the area, Calvin was able to escape the normal meet and greets that would have come with territory of any new relationship.

His family was conveniently located out of town and his job at Delta Airlines seemed to keep our weekends confined to dinners in the city and other seemingly normal romantic date-like occasions.

Calvin was an excellent planner. Remembering the scripted voicemail and the deliberate way he would say my name, he was no different when it came to any outing of any variety.

Everything had to be a production, timed to the millisecond, and rehearsed. Back then, it was a relief to not have to plan things myself and, with my busy schedule as a Manager, I encouraged any amount of help Calvin was willing to give me.

Providing some structure to a night on the town seemed harmless enough to me at the time. He would argue that reservations in his name were necessary even for lunch on a sub shop on the weekend.

It didn't dawn on me back then, that his need to be announced at every establishment might be an indicator of another problem.

He seemed almost too eager to "educate" me on the high-society culture that would await our date nights. "Demetria, let me educate you on what is in store for you this evening." While I hated his use of the word "educate," I appreciated what seemed to be his thoughtfulness in wanting to prepare me.

Back then, I made the conscious choice to excuse his use of the word "educate" and opted to rely on what appeared to be his good intentions. Little did I know, those good intentions were cloaked in a maliciousness no one could have predicted, especially a good natured person like myself...

In my estimation, I was someone who had paid her dues and had earned the right to appreciate the finer things in life.

Vividly, I remembered the times in my childhood when my father would leave us to our own devices. Time that was supposed to contain happy memories was, instead, dark and desperate as we were forced to eat baby-food because my father was always too drunk or messed up to hold down a job. Providing food for the family took a backseat to whatever crisis he had conjured up next.

The expertly manicured ways of this sophisticated gentleman, however, lured me into a calculating dance of control that would sneak up on me like a fog. Unlike my father, Calvin seemed to take pride in taking care of things and in the early days, when everything was bright and shiny and new, Calvin assured me that my days of shouldering 100% of my family's burden were officially over.

Dinners at some of the top restaurants in Atlanta were intended to mesmerize me, ultimately distracted me from the truth that lurked beneath Calvin's cool and calm exterior. Mr. Smooth had the dating routine down and I would play his perfect victim.

My own lifestyle had left me tired, weary, and vulnerable to the machinations of a man who needed a "lady" to make him whole.

I would give him a layer of real credibility that his job at Delta Airlines couldn't provide him. Little did I know, in Calvin's mind, my willingness to be his "perfect" girlfriend would help him with his other lies, lies that validated "Jones Enterprises." I would become his pawn as he played games with a gullible world who was just begging to believe a smooth and sophisticated gentleman with "standards."

The busy sounds of a Friday night bustling with Atlanta's finest urban high-rollers welcomed a wide eyed me who was eager to experience every drop it had to offer. The light dancing across the skyscrapers was similar to the light reflecting off of Calvin's eyes the night I first met him only one week ago.

I had maintained the traditional 3 day hold before calling him as calling any sooner would surely show my overly-eager hand. I didn't have to make his dating me as easy as he had it at McDonalds. At work, I was required to be available at the customer's beck and call.

My private life though was a different story and it was my choice to play it my way. I was determined to hold at least some of the cards even if I didn't completely understand the game.

Being a single mom who had earned every cent of my lifestyle, dating had never been a priority for me so Friday nights like this Friday night with Calvin were rare to say the least.

So far, Calvin was scoring perfect 10's. Arriving to pick me up, he was ten minutes early so that he could put fresh flowers in a vase for me prior to whisking me off to dinner downtown. He even bought a bouquet for my mother. When he opened the door to his Charger for me, I chuckled at how the moment seemed like it had been pulled straight out of the Dodge commercials on TV.

We were the idyllic couple on a first date, in a fantastically sexy car set against Atlanta's electrically charged skyline. My heart pounded with fear and adrenaline as Calvin methodically ducked and weaved through the remainder of rush hour traffic. The high-end Bose sound system thundered and pulsed loudly, competing with Calvin's lesson about what was in store for me that evening.

Reaching over to lower the volume so that I could better hear him, one of his expertly manicured hands batted mine away from a seemingly never-ending panel of knobs.

"Nah, lil' lady! Those aren't for little girl hands."

Turning the volume down a hair, he dramatically focused on the decibel indicator as if he knew precisely what frequency would work for the surrounding landscape.

"Now, as I was saying... Damon's Steakhouse is the place to be seen if you are anybody to be respected here in Atlanta Demetria."

He tucked the Charger into one of the larger parking spots in an underground parking lot of one of Atlanta's most prestigious sky-scrapers.

He went on, "I'm surprised you haven't been here before. Oh! Actually, my bad, it's not like you would have come here yourself. There aren't too many eligible guys like me in your neighborhood to take you places like I can. Let's go have some fun!" Somehow Calvin had a knack for complimenting and offending at the very same time.

Turning the thunderous engine of his prized possession off, he methodically wiped down the front console and steering wheel of any lingering fingerprints in an attempt to, as he put it, "make things feel brand new." I wondered how horrified this man would be with the condition of my Honda.

Half-full packages of ketchup and greasy fingerprints were sure to meet him at every corner of a vehicle that I had once considered my second-home. Calvin was also quick which made any attempt at analyzing this man and his intentions, virtually impossible. Before I could even think my thought or respond to his question, he continued, "It's important that you understand how to be seen with me. I mean, most women just don't know how to BE with a man these days."

Calvin had made his way to my side of the car where I stood. He dramatically shrunk his shoulders in disgust. "Do you see what I'm talkin' about? I mean I'm gonna try to tell it to ya' nice, so I hope you hear me. Let me open the door for you and I mean EVERY door because you'll embarrass me if you don't... and we wouldn't want THAT, would we?"

I had never met a man before who had so many rules and guidelines about every-day life. Still on the fence about whether his rules and guidelines were really necessary, I played along by giving him a dose of his own medicine.

"Oh, I see, Calvin, I was thinking I'd be embarrassing YOU by expecting too much out of my date by waitin' on you."

The challenge that had first made its appearance during our introduction in the McDonald's dining room was making yet another appearance tonight in the ritzy VIP parking lot of Damon's Steakhouse.

Grabbing my hand and guiding me through the restaurant's lobby Calvin went on, "No, unfortunately Demetria, folks will think that you are one of those common school-yard chicks tryin' to be a boy in a man's world. Well, I've gotta message for you. I don't hang with those kinds of bitches. That's why I'm trying to educate you on some standards."

My hand still in his, he squeezed it especially hard upon saying the last word, "standards." I would come to learn about these "standards" like people learn about the Ten Commandments. In Calvin's case though, the list of "standards" could fill the Library of Congress.

Concerned at first by his firm grasp, he released my hand, gathered me into his arms and pecked me on the forehead whispering, "okay, enough of that for now."

His hair and eyes glistened under the twinkle-lights of the Damon's Steakhouse awning.

While some red flags were certainly in attendance, Calvin was unlike any man I had ever met before. "Maybe these 'standards' are why this man had become successful in the first place." I thought.

I would get busy convincing myself of all sorts of things that night, as people in the surrounding tables at the restaurant seemed to gaze at us like we were the African American version of Ken and Barbie. Setting my concerns about his "standards" aside for the time being, I allowed myself to enjoy the attention Calvin's standards seemed to be awarding him.

His suede, silk lined blazer was the perfect shade of beige. Calvin's wardrobe seemed to contrast perfectly with the table napkins and accent linens while I couldn't help but wonder if his matching was merely a coincidence or perhaps a more deliberate conclusion. I could smell just the right amount of men's cologne as we approached our table.

Of course Calvin attended to assisting me into my seat while at the same time surveying the room with a casual elegance reserved for English princes. "It is obvious this man has been here before," I thought to myself. Reaching across the table for my hands, Calvin ran his thumbs over the top of my fingers and matched my gaze for what seemed like an eternity.

"I can tell that you are way out of your league here Demetria, but I assure you, you are in good hands."

Calvin delivered meticulously calculating blows to my self-esteem in what appeared to be an exquisitely romantic moment to the rest of the room. I wondered if anyone could have imagined what he had just said to me. Blushing in a fit of embarrassment, I pulled my hands away from Calvin's and back into my lap.

Laughing and nodding his head, he went on, "no, no! Don't be like that, you got nothin' to hide, right? You have plenty of time to learn and who better to teach you, than me? Awe, c'mon Demetria, you aren't going to be like that and spoil my fun now are you?"

Amazingly, this man knew how to make a recovery. In perfect Houdini style, he was able to fish my hands out from their burial place under the napkin on my lap. With the same goofy puppy look he had used at the McDonalds, he was able to retrieve my sense of humor before it desperately fell into the deep abyss.

Apparently Calvin could behave in whatever way he wanted in this over-the top cushy restaurant while I would have to await his further "instruction."

However, since this was our first date, I remembered some advice my mother had bestowed upon me as I was getting ready. She insisted that I take a minute to loosen up and have fun instead of taking everything so seriously. "Let the man entertain you honey! It's YOUR TURN!"

My mother seemed to be having a great time living vicariously through our new romance. It delighted me to see her enjoying a relationship that was so far from anything she had ever experienced.

Rifling through my cosmetic bag, my mother delighted in selecting various lipstick shades of magenta, plum, and other colors that corresponded with wardrobe choices that I hoped would make the perfect impression.

After hours of deliberation, my mother dramatically selected the boldest of the shades in contention, "Boysenberry Charade." I wondered how cosmetic companies came up with these names anyway. It dawned on me that maybe my mother picked this shade for its name and not REALLY because it was the perfect hue.

Not one to particularly enjoy primping, I didn't give it another thought and focused most of my attention on which pieces of her vintage jewelry would work best with what was becoming my mother's ensemble.

I wondered if Calvin was appreciating any of our hard work and effort. Before I was able to entertain anymore of his observations on my lack of experience, a waiter by the name of Alexandre arrived with a nametag that identified him as a sommelier.

"Hello, my name is Alexandre and I will be your sommelier for this evening. If you have any questions, I am here to explain your options..." This young man looked like he was ripped right out of a GQ magazine and like a court jester dramatically presented a leather bound list of wines and other beverages.

Drumming up some courage to take this Alexandre up on his offer to answer any of our questions, I asked "What is a sommelier?" Struggling through the pronunciation Calvin replied, "You don't know what a sommelier is?"

Disgusted with me, he turned to Alexandre muttering, "Don't worry Alex(whoever you are), we've got this handled. Give me the list and I'll walk this big mouth through her 'options.'"

Before Alexandre could hand the leather bound list to me, Calvin swiped it out of his hands and waved him away. "In fact, send Christine over here, I asked for her to handle my table tonight anyway. I don't know what you are even doing here."

Embarrassed about being called out in front of the entire restaurant, Alexandre shuffled away and toward the kitchen while Calvin focused his infuriated attention back onto me.

"I will give you one chance to apologize to me for flirting with that waiter while on a date with me."

Not believing what I was hearing, the restaurant was quickly becoming a beautifully staged nightmare. Our date was feeling more and more like a soap opera as people at neighboring tables tried to pretend they were eating their dinners. Feeling like an actor on a set, I felt the heaviness of the room and the overwhelming expectation to keep my composure.

Not at all unlike the scene that played out during our first introduction, I really had to wonder if it was just me, or maybe I was the one who had lost my marbles. How in the world could Calvin think I was flirting with the waiter?

"I was not flirting with the waiter. I was simply asking him a question." I whispered calmly. "I would never flirt with someone else while on a date with you."

I hoped Calvin would tone it down a few notches and reached out for his hands like he had reached out for mine just moments ago.
Instead of letting me have them he pulled

both of his hands back saying, "You don't get these yet dear. You have some work to do."

Seeing Christine, the waitress assigned to our table, hiding behind the bar on the opposite side of the restaurant, Calvin motioned her over with a nod of his head. Customers had gone back to their own dinners while I struggled with what to do next.

On the off-chance he really did think I was flirting with the sommelier, I managed a few compliments in Calvin's direction just to reassure him of my intentions. "I was really excited about our date tonight. You really made quite an impression on me."

Fumbling with the linen napkin on my lap, I did my best to change the subject and found asking him questions about his career and Jones Enterprises the safest route to go.

Calvin seemed proud of his work at Delta and loved telling stories about his rise to the top of a baggage handling industry that was rife with conflict and public scrutiny.

After 9-11, his work in a field that demanded change and accountability at break-neck speed, Calvin was rewarded for his unyielding eye for detail.

While other terminals saw layoffs and turnover in droves, he was able to not only hang on, but get promoted through the security and baggage ranks with unquestionable ease.

Noticing his comfort and delight in this part of the conversation, I was able to enjoy listening to a man who needed to be in charge.

This man knew how to tell a story and for that, I was grateful as my gaze settled on the romantic skyline. Damon's restaurant hosted panoramic views of an Atlanta I yearned to experience. "Could I get that experience with Mr. Smooth?" I asked myself.

Before I could ask myself anymore questions, the waitress, Christine, had finally made it to our table and was able to take our order.

Sensing Calvin's need to take the reins, I let him order for me and appreciated the new calmness that had embarked on what had started out as a tumultuous date. Clearly not a two way street, Calvin was not fearful about flirting with this Pamela Anderson look-a-like.

The epitome of bold, he complimented her on her new hairdo while asking her how her classes at the University were coming along. He had obviously been here before.

While I could still see and feel the pressure of his expectations regarding my every move, proceeding with caution seemed to be my best bet if I wanted to make the most of 'our' evening. I knew better than to bring his hypocrisy to his attention and opted for my best game face. Rewarding me for not reacting to his flirtatious demeanor with the waitress, he leaned over the table and kissed my hands.

Calvin would go on to do his best that night. He too was looking for some certainty in a world that seemed resigned to victimize him. Telling me that his survival was contingent on predicting when the next shoe would drop, I found some empathy for a man who seemed to appreciate structure over compromise.

"I can be the one to compromise..." I thought, "If it meant a lifestyle like this and if standards REALLY did mean some amount of peace of mind, maybe I could follow some rules."

Calvin seemed to pride himself on educating me at every turn. From the way I held my steak knife to how I folded my napkin in my lap instead of all balled up, I let him "take care of me" as Calvin liked to put it. I hated letting anyone "take care of me" but somehow, something about the promise of this new life, encouraged me to make Calvin an exception.

While warning signs may have been in abundance, they paled in comparison to the boring and monotonous life I wanted so desperately to run from. A little fire wouldn't prevent me from getting everything I wanted out of this life. Having come from the fire myself, I knew better than anyone how to tame it. At least that is what I had convinced myself. My self-confidence could handle just about anything and I relied on my good judgment to get me out of any predicament.

This Calvin seemed harmless enough by the end of our first dinner date. I convinced myself to give Mr. Smooth a chance despite his bullish ways, since he seemed like the only one who held the ticket to my destiny.

4

STANDARDS

Destiny is seldom perfect and largely a matter of perspective when playing your hand at dating so late in life. This wasn't my first rodeo. With one eyebrow critically raised, I watched Calvin fold his t-shirts with a cardboard insert so that each fold was measured to the millimeter.

He would attempt to put the military to shame as he methodically assembled piles of t-shirts, underwear and jeans in an attempt to educate me on the "standards" that would be sure to keep him happy while staying at my household.

After weeks of courting me with nights on the town, he had eased his way into my chaotic work schedule by convincing me to stay over at my place more often than not. At first, it was nice to have someone other than my boys to come home to and I looked forward to providing Calvin with some stability that only a domestic life could offer him.

I settled into the role Calvin insisted he needed out of me. Having come from an abuse story of his own, he would recount a childhood where he was largely ignored by his mother and incessantly criticized by his father.

Not being able to count on anything consistently nurturing from either one of them, Calvin found a way to survive on his own and developed a survival strategy that included a structured but isolated autonomous existence.

Friends were in short supply as he struggled with what he described as their loyalty issues and, in many cases, most friends could not handle his rigid management style of everything from where they should shop for groceries to how they should parent their kids.

Trying to empathize with the man, I forced myself to learn as many of his "standards" as I could. With my own hectic work schedule, weekday nights that were once my kids' were now lessons at the hands of a man who swore he meant well.

Handing the cardboard insert to me, Calvin instructed me to reproduce his work with the t-shirts. "Really?" I muttered.

"Is this really necessary? I just watched you do it Calvin." I expertly folded the t-shirt just like he had all of the other ones. "Good job, but you failed on attitude." he stated, taking the insert out of my hands and throwing it against my newly painted bedroom wall, he proclaimed, "Lesson over."

Unfolding the t-shirts that were already folded to his liking, he released them to every corner of my bedroom just to make sure he got his point across. I was delirious from double shifts at McDonalds that week and folding t-shirts to precision for Calvin was simply not on my radar of priorities.

Taking a place in the center of my bed, the irony of his still having shoes on was not lost on me. He went on, "You see, until you realize that this is a matter of respect and NOT about the damn t-shirts, we are going to CONTINUE to have issues and that's your choice, not mine Demetria."

I hated how he used my name in sentences like I was some kind of child.

Now nearly six months into the relationship, I had grown accustomed to Calvin's temper tantrums and learned to avoid them by playing along with his various tests and routines. Nearly every mundane task required an exaggerated process of checks and balances that, at first, was helpful.

In the early days of me and Calvin, my world consisted of randomized chaos.

I didn't have the luxury to put a process to anything much less the way I cleaned a countertop. The thought of organizing a drawer full of plastic bags by size and type seemed like overkill in a world where my value as a parent had more to do with what shoes I could afford my boys than it did my kitchen organizing capabilities.

"You see, it's not just about the dishwasher Demetria, it's about the way you think. When you think random, you get random. Plain and simple." While some of his suggestions proved useful, most were overkill and felt like a self-inflated attempt at stroking an ego that had never been truly checked. He had his mom to thank for that.

Not having the emotional stamina to cope with the demands of an unruly Calvin, he got his way most, if not all, of the time.

Because it was so difficult to achieve any kind of praise from her husband, Calvin's mom sought the approval of her son. Encouraging him at every turn, even the turns that were questionable at best, she unwittingly created the very man that stood before me, a man who got amusement out of berating me about how I had unloaded the dishwasher.

"I told you 'Unload the bottom first so the water from the top doesn't soak everything beneath.' Why you can't remember that, tells me a lot about how little you respect me." It was 6am on a Tuesday morning. The boys were with their dad that week, the week Calvin had successfully convinced me to move in entirely.

Against my better judgment, I caved to a man who knew how to turn on his puppy-dog charm more often than he would annoy me. I remember a conversation with my mom in the days prior, where she suggested his charm and sophistication might be a welcome change for the entire family.

Recounting Calvin's various attempts at winning her over, my mom loved how he noticed that the jewelry I was wearing on our first date was really hers and not mine. "You can't blame a man for having some standards, honey" she implored to my soft-side in ways that worked to his benefit.

"Do you know how many women would die for a man to care that much about anything in their lives much less the way her kitchen should be organized?"

Rolling my eyes while backed into the corner of my kitchen counter, Calvin removed the remaining glasses and coffee mugs from the top of the dishwasher, intentionally spilling water onto the dishes below.

"SEE! Do I have to show you the cause and effect here?" He was more irritated than usual this morning. Slamming the top tray closed, he started removing the larger dishes. Now wet, he shoved plate after plate into my hands with a fury greater than I what I was used to out of him.

My hands, now overflowing with the wet dishes yielded an even bigger disaster. Not having any room to deliver the dishes safely to the counter, two of the slippery dishes fell out of my hands, shattering onto the kitchen floor.

"You see! That's what happens when you don't give a shit about your stuff! YOU DID THIS, happy now?!

Beads of sweat were staining his newly dry cleaned dress shirt from Nordstrom. I was petrified about what he might do upon the realization I had spoiled his newest purchase.

"Do I have to do everything for you?" Pulling the silverware out in its compartment, he threw the entire thing across the kitchen where it exploded on the kitchen table. Pulling the remaining dishes and bowls out of the dishwasher, he threw each across the room with an unbridled and escalating rage that exceeded the previous item.

With each explosion against the kitchen table and walls, he shouted, "Is this better? It's your choice Demetria. It's time you learned a little bit about respect. Because, if you can't respect your things, you certainly can't respect ME."

Slamming the front of the dishwasher closed, he cornered me with each of his hulking arms and squashed his knee into my groin until I couldn't breathe.

"No wonder you didn't have a man when I found you. You couldn't keep a man to save your life. It's just like your mom said." His presence was overwhelming in what was now the tiniest corner of my kitchen.

The expectations of a "generous" man just trying to help achieve order in my house would enhance my mom's insistence that it was Calvin who was Mr. Right.

"I'm sorry..." I trembled with the weight of everyone else's expectations that morning, realizing that fighting him would only prove futile. Releasing me from the crushing force of his knee, he drew his hand back and slapped me across the face as hard as he could. Tears raced to the finish line of what would be the first of his many attempts to shame and humiliate me in my own household.

Shuttering to the bone in regret, it dawned on me that the house I had worked myself to the bone for could now be considered rightfully his. By giving him the green-light, I had willingly made it that way.

"This is MY house now too Demetria and it be best you start showing me some RESPECT."

5
TYRANNY

Calvin always had a way to sweeten his rotten behavior. Because of his job at United, he was constantly given free or discounted tickets to "destinations" that promised a new start and another chance for me to redeem myself. Somehow, he had convinced me that his rage and control issues were a result of my misbehavior and not because of any inherent problems with his DNA profile. Like a surgeon, he expertly carved into arguments my mother had used against me for years.

He promised me that with his help, I could become the daughter my mother had always dreamed of having.

Prior to Calvin, the thought of my being any less than her pride and joy was as foreign to me as some of the elaborate trips Calvin would plan. Like clockwork, he would present me with tickets to Vegas and Salt Lake City in an attempt to keep me in line.

Episodes like that Tuesday morning over how to load the dishwasher were becoming all too common as his attempt to take over my life was now becoming more than just a nagging concern. Partnering with my mom would be his way of justifying his various means of "helping" me.

Playing with the clasp on a new diamond tennis bracelet he had given me just a week ago, I welcomed the warmth shining through my kitchen window on one of my rare moments of solitude and reflection. Calvin was on yet another trip. Since I had taken on a new afternoon shift, this particular Sunday morning was left open just for me.

The diamonds twinkled in the early-morning light and teased me into believing, one more time, that Calvin might really feel remorse for his controlling ways.

More often than not, my only mornings alone were spent balancing Calvin's conduct with his means of restitution.

Running my fingers over the diamonds, I watched their shiny shadows dance on the walls of the kitchen nook.

I remembered coming home from work early one afternoon to not so subtle changes by a man who was insistent on making his mark and claiming his territory.

Walls that once welcomed me with a warm periwinkle blue were now a deep angry red. Pictures that had been in my family for years were banished to a dark corner of the basement while pictures of muscle cars and Malcom X movie posters screamed at me that someone new was in charge.

This new dictator was someone I had willingly taken in and now that he had taken my mom under his wing, he would be even more successful than I ever could have realized.

In response to Calvin's re-decorating and painting, my mom would defend him by insisting that he had every right to make my house his home. "How would you feel if you moved into his home, dear? You've gotta let a man be a man or he'll be snitting around elsewhere." She fidgeted with her keychain as if to re-direct any of her nervous energy onto an inanimate object that couldn't argue back.

She seemed more concerned about Calvin leaving me than she did about my standing my ground. I couldn't bring myself to blame her though. Her history was so very different than mine.

Her fear of my father determined everything she did and didn't do. It was my choice to not fill her in on the physical nature of Calvin's assault on my life.

His takeover had been gradual and full of "nice" things that my father never even attempted to do. In my mom's mind, Calvin was a better man because of his desire to maintain unachievable standards. Apparently there was hope in a flawed man who insisted he meant well.

While taking my mom's advice with a grain of salt, I couldn't help but wonder if Calvin indeed meant well and made sure to do everything I could to decipher his true intent from what I thought might be his more sinister motives to control and take over what I had spent a lifetime achieving.

Upon the first signs of trouble, Calvin was meticulous about distracting me from my very genuine feelings of doubt and onto the logistics of "free" vacations that only he could provide because of his work with the airline.

After weeks of double shifts and maneuvering my children's school and sports schedules, the thought of a REAL vacation outweighed any of my growing concerns.

I was able to keep a handle on Calvin by gushing over everything he offered, even when what he offered wasn't really free. Since extravagance always took priority over frugality, Calvin would lose sight of things like rental cars, hotels, and the activities HE would want to do once we got there.

My idea of a vacation included time off of my feet and not being held hostage to a schedule. He would argue that my lazy thinking and lazy ways were the reasons I had not achieved a lifestyle as grand as his.

Insisting he book every ounce of time at museums and shows, Calvin would guilt me into using my credit card on these trips by professing a dwindling budget. Arguing the gifts he had given me were now taking a toll on his bank account, I submitted to his guilt in order to avoid any additional drama.

Shifting my gaze from the bracelet's reflection on the wall and back onto the reality of what now sat on my wrist, I recalled how stunned I was by his purchase. No one had ever purchased a gift like this for me before.

If only Calvin's intentions were as transparent as the diamonds that seemed to be my only real company these days.

The bracelet I had never asked for would now serve as powerful ammunition that he could use at will, or whenever he needed my surrender.

On exhausting nights after work, when all I wanted to do was sleep, Calvin would remind me of his sacrifice while insisting I find "ways" to thank him.

Wearing lingerie he had purchased for me that was far beyond my comfort zone, my naturally aching body begged for a reprieve but none would come in the face of what I owed him.

Desperate to measure up to his expectations, I allowed him to turn on videos of females half my age in an attempt to show my willingness to satisfy him. Performing acts I had a hard time faking, much less stomaching, I made peace with girls who were old enough to be my daughter.

Secretly, I was grateful to leave the work to them. On my stomach, I watched what he did with no reaction. Prodding me to participate, I would oblige with, "Oh, yeah… that's hot" until he surrendered to his own version of "sweet" reverie.

Grateful on the nights he came quickly, I justified my actions as the actions of a woman who was strong enough to face reality. No longer was I the twenty-something of men's fantasies. Instead of fighting, I felt that my choice to go along would bring some amount of peace and, for the time being, it seemed our arrangement was working.

More like a barter or trade agreement, I wondered how my mom was able to manage such a one-sided arrangement with my father.

So, in honor of her sacrifice, I managed to push the dirtier truths of Calvin's propensities in the bedroom aside and concentrate on the things he WAS trying to bring to my table.

Now nearly a year into our relationship, I had learned which battles to fight and opted to be happy for my mom, a lady who had never even been to Disney World, much less experience the excitement and bright lights of a place like Atlantic City.

On at least two occasions when Calvin's trips collided with my schedule, my mom was invited to go on "the trip of a lifetime" in my place. I wondered how much of a coincidence it was that some of these trips were booked on the busiest weeks at the restaurant. Calvin would adamantly insist he had no control over the dates and destinations.

Resigned to my peace-making purpose I chose to be happy for the reprieve. My mom would return home downright giddy, with wild stories of winning games of Black Jack while recounting stories of seeing famous talk-show hosts or celebrities in the lobby of the hotel they were staying at.

More often than not, trips would culminate into him leaving her at some over-the-top spa for day treatments while he enjoyed "innocent", more adult styled "entertainment," I would only learn about upon receipt of my monthly credit card bill.

Calvin would argue his afternoons at the strip-club were necessary because he was clearly not getting any love and respect at home.

"What difference does it make?" he would claim, "you lettum' into the bedroom."

Not considering that porn was the gateway drug to escorts and strippers, I would come to learn another valuable lesson at the hands of a man who was supposed to love me. I learned that he was more than capable of using my good intentions against me in an effort to cure his own guilty conscience.

Any worry about Calvin's expenses on these trips was outweighed by the peace of mind that came from having my house back to myself.

"Besides," I thought to myself, "he's going with my mom, how much trouble can he get into anyway?" Even in the cases where he would charge my credit card to its limit, there wasn't really anything I could do about it.

Calvin would make sure to cry on my mother's shoulder at my every hint of discontent, leaving me to assume the bad guy role time and time again.

"He's a troubled man Demetria, but that doesn't mean you just throw him away. I didn't throw your father away."

My mom struggled to make sense of a relationship that she refused was anything like the relationship she had with my dad. I was equally as unwilling to spoil the idealistic view my mom had of Calvin and agreed to take a week off of work to go on what would be our first trip to Orlando.

The Orlando trip and bracelet would be the olive branch Calvin would extend for the dishwasher incident but his version of an olive branch was beginning to feel more like a Venus flytrap these days than a true attempt at reconciliation.

Frustrated with a diamond bracelet that should have delighted me, I tugged at the clasp in hopes to be free from his control.

Ridiculing myself for thinking that removing the bracelet would liberate me, I allowed fear to keep it in place as it dangled over the kitchen table and over the fresh grooves made by the silverware he had thrown just over a week ago.

The reflection of the diamonds were no longer smooth and predictable as the light seemed to crack and shatter in his wake. Too afraid of what Calvin might do if I damaged the bracelet, I refrained from letting it crash to the floor.

Instead I would make a mental note, remembering a solitary moment in a kitchen that was no longer mine, a damaged kitchen table and a fractured me. I would remember a moment when I disgusted myself for being more fearful of a man than I was of God.

6

JAILBAIT & ME

"When was the last time you were treated to a vacation?" Calvin turned on the lightshow that never failed him. Eyes blazing, he leaned over the kitchen island, practically diving into the salad I was making for dinner. "Um, I dunno. I guess I took the boys to the beach a few summers ago but I'm not sure if that counts or not." I responded, scooping out a handful of grated cheese for the salad.

Calvin grabbed the package out of my hands before I could proceed. Closing the zipped pouch like a guard locking a prison cell he blurted, "Is THAT how you're going to get ready for our trip?

You think THAT'S gonna help with your bathing suit issues?"

Calvin taunted me about the cheese in an attempt to thwart my well-deserved appetite.

Longer shifts at work didn't necessarily mean longer lunch breaks. In fact, because of the new addition of an arcade to the movie theater across the street, increased traffic meant my skipping lunch altogether. I simply couldn't risk the trainees getting something wrong and jeopardizing my job, the only thing I felt I had going for myself these days.

As a result, it seemed trainees were getting more time off than I was these days. It was a miracle that Noelle had managed to stay on despite my complaints and warnings of health code violations should she continue on my team. Coming to work like she had just come home from the club probably did her more favors than I was willing to realize. While her relationship with the french-fry sleeves would continue to be an ongoing problem, her relationship with my boss seemed to be the solution.

Instead of citing Noelle for her uniform shirts being two sizes too small, my boss would give her the green-light, time and time again. On one particularly humiliating occasion, my boss sounding more like Calvin reminded me,

"Don't worry about Noelle. If she wasn't doing something right, she wouldn't be here. You should just concentrate on what YOU do."

Not being one to have to be told twice, I dropped the subject of Noelle's uniforms entirely and opted to stick to my guns when it came to recurrent complaints about the way she handled the food. Worried about what might go down upon the new arcade's Grand Opening, I managed to convince my boss not to schedule her for that entire weekend.

It was THAT weekend would be the weekend I would finally have a chance to manage my life my way. Remembering the Sunday morning in my kitchen nook, I recalled a great morning of reflection that allowed a clearer perspective on my life and purpose.

Mornings like that were few and far between as life with Calvin made worshipping any other God impossible. Missing church on that Sunday, I regretted all of the Sundays I missed as a result of my relationship with a lesser man. In those early morning hours I made an agreement with God privately in hopes something would change.

Returning to work that afternoon, after my agreement with God, I felt more in control and more purposeful than ever. With Calvin on his trip and Noelle nowhere in sight, a great peace and predictability came over my day.

I didn't have to worry that I was getting another something wrong with a man who couldn't see how hard I was trying. At work, I didn't have to worry that my job was being jeopardized by some teen who didn't know one thing about struggle. All she had to do was show up at work with her barely-there uniform to be taken seriously. It wasn't too hard for me to imagine this hot mess being one of the girls I fell asleep to on nights when Calvin was at home.

Forcing myself to get back to attending my salad, I presumed Calvin might give his volatile episodes a rest considering all of my allowances in the bedroom and for my ability to turn a blind-eye on his extra-curricular activities while away on trips. A few weeks had gone by since receiving my lesson about unloading the dishwasher and he was fresh off a trip to the coast.

"Or, do I just not matter to you?" Calvin continued. When I failed at his rules, he would consistently reason that I just didn't care about him.

More often than not, my failure at following his rules had more to do with my memory and the volumes of detail I had to retain on his behalf. The fact I was even attempting to follow his rules should have been his first clue that I cared about him.

Instead, his ego would lead him to believe otherwise. I started wondering if my "not caring about him," gave him leverage to keep on controlling me.

Attempting to grab the cheese back out of his hands, he caught me by my wrist and squeezed tightly so that I knew who was in charge. I wasn't going to back down this time. "My bathing suit issues are none of your concern and if you didn't matter to me, you wouldn't be going on the trip."

I calmly tried to reason with him in hopes he would release me from his grasp and let me resume with my dinner. Squeezing my wrist even tighter, the tiny diamonds from my bracelet burrowed into my skin like razors, causing broken blood vessels I would have to find a way to hide later.

Wincing, I tried to pull back with no luck. In the same tone he used when reciting my name when I met him, Calvin sarcastically corrected me, "You wouldn't be taking ME on the trip?

I think you must be mistaken young lady. I am the one who is taking YOU on this trip. Without ME, YOU wouldn't be going ANYWHERE." Slamming my hand into the salad bowl between us, lettuce leaves and carrot slices flew everywhere.

Any illusion of a romantic trip with this man would now be as foreign to me as a trip to the Moon as he dumped the entire package of cheese on the floor.

"Whatcha' gonna do now Demetria? Is this the way you treat a man who is about to take you on a trip of a lifetime? You eat what I tell you you're going to eat. I'm not gonna take your nasty ass on some nice vacation if you've been gettin' into the cheese. Now, clean this mess YOU made NOW and get back to making an appropriate dinner."

Ignoring my throbbing wrists, I hesitated putting myself in an even more compromising position by assuming a role on the floor. While my hesitation would only last an instant, in Calvin's world, it was an eternity. Any delay or perceived questioning of his authority, especially during moments like these, was the kiss of death.

"What are you waiting for woman? You gonna keep on disrespecting ME?" Losing all sense of decorum, Calvin grabbed me by the back of the hair and forced me to my knees. Shoving my face into the cheese and the floor, my mind raced to the day I moved in. I was so proud of myself. This would be the first place I ever owned.

Nothing thrilled me more than the house's bright shiny hardwood floors.

Unlike the cheap, disposable laminate flooring that was typical of most of the apartments I lived in, the permanence of these hardwoods seemed to promise a sturdier, more predictable future.

In these horrid moments, I regretted having ever taken this promise for granted. Sobbing uncontrollably, my crying would only be met with Calvin's version of empathy.

"I know honey, sometimes I have to get mean. You make me that way. It's seems to be the only way to get your ATTENTION. How can I expect you to respect me if I am not clear about THE RULES?"

With each end to a sentence, Calvin would lift and grind my face deeper into the mess on the floor. Too afraid to do anything, I did as he directed. In silent agony, I picked up croutons and carrot shavings while he cleaned the entire refrigerator out of anything that could be deemed appetizing.

"We're doing this to help you, Demetria. Your mother and I agree that you need to start re-prioritizing your attention and that I should come before the cheese."

It's funny what your mind does during moments like this. My face was pounding from the impact on the floor as I wondered if Noelle had ever experienced anything like this before.

Allowing myself to submit to the dark and bitter places I never would have thought to venture, I wondered if girls like Noelle got to bypass episodes like this because they are hot. Perhaps jailbait doesn't get punished because they are willing to be jailbait.

For the first time in my life, I questioned my foundation. A foundation I thought was supported and rewarded by God. I wondered why, after all of this sacrifice, why God would be testing me now. My throbbing cheek now sounded like a tribal drum as it echoed the self-doubts I spent a lifetime ignoring.

"What if I got it wrong?"

My conscience played games with my soul in those moments. I assaulted myself with questions as the light from the refrigerator served as a spotlight for the interrogation. "Maybe I deserve this. Maybe, this is my punishment for not going along with society's rules. Perhaps, they are really God's rules after all." Beaten to the core, I questioned a God that could let this happen to me.

Why would HE abandon me?

Amidst my attempts at answering that question, I surrendered to a man and his principles that night, while my mom's voice echoed loudly in the background, "Your father never did anything that nice for me."

7

ORLANDO

Believe me, I was questioning my own sanity on the morning we checked luggage and egos onto the Delta Airlines flight that would take us to Orlando for my "trip of a lifetime." The only glimmer of hope that remained after Calvin's latest tirade over cheese was the evidence he left behind by-way of my swollen and bruised right cheek. This evidence would serve as the only time Calvin would be left with some explaining to do.

Relieved that I finally had some ammunition of my own, I readied myself for what I was preparing would be the fight of a lifetime.

This fight wouldn't be one against any man or less-than man like Calvin, but rather a fight with myself and a fight for clarity in my dealings with God. Understanding Calvin's logic was the easy part shockingly enough. Over the year plus ordeal, it became easier to predict his tantrums.

Kneeling in the light of the refrigerator, scrambling for answers as to why God would put me in this position, I discovered more questions than answers.

These questions would serve as my fuel for a trip I wanted desperately NOT to take. Pleading with God to make my path clear, I would only be faced with dead-end streets.

In conversations down the hall, I heard a Calvin I didn't recognize talking to a mom who didn't know any better. Or did she? In her own way, she had reconciled that Calvin's actions were those of a man who could be redeemed. She was in her own way, trying to help me. Convinced of Calvin's good intentions, I heard her counsel a man who was beyond help.

It was touching in an odd way, my mom, in, way over her head, but meaning well like she always did. Calvin was also out of his element, as there was absolutely zero justification for his hitting me. He was now the one on the defensive and doing some scrambling of his own.

He would have to top the famed tennis bracelet which would be no easy task. Thankfully for him, the bruising faded quickly but the mark it would leave on his credibility with my mom was yet to be seen. The trip to Orlando would become our testing ground. Our future would depend on his ability to make amends for what he had done and I had given my mom my word that I would give him a chance.

Somehow, knowing that I had some amount of control over the outcome, gave me the added self-confidence for the long flight and days ahead.

Of course I wondered why even this measure was necessary. I knew in my heart that this less-than-a-man wasn't for me and no trip to Orlando was going to change that fact.

There are times in life when you are so done with the path you have willingly taken that you will do ANYTHING to ensure a new route. Equipped with the oversized shades Calvin had once deemed 'obnoxious,' I hid from the man who had made such a mess of me. Knowing better than to criticize me at this crucial point in the trip, Calvin sulked in his seat by the window while I enjoyed the much-needed privacy I claimed for myself.

For a minute, I allowed myself to relax, knowing that I had the upper-hand against someone who was supposed to be the love of my life. My mind appreciated the temporary reprieve as it wandered to the sympathetic expressions on my co-workers faces when they saw the damage Mr. Smooth had done to my face. Having not made it a practice to share the details of my personal life with those I managed, it came as a huge surprise to all but Noelle.

Out of all the employees at the restaurant, she would be the one with the most questions, the most feedback, and the most concern but instead, she seemed unfazed as she refused to make eye-contact with me and opted to take on extra duties that would keep her occupied.

With the trip to Orlando only days away, getting prepared to leave took priority over Noelle's strange behavior that week. I just chalked it up to an immature girl who felt uncomfortable with the brutal reality my face forced her to see.

It wasn't like I really wanted to be sharing life's lessons with her anyway. It seemed like life was going just fine for her. Apparently she was the first of the trainees to have earned a paid vacation.

Somehow, her conflict resolution skills with the patrons was earning her high marks that translated into benefits and bonuses I never had the chance of experiencing as a manager. Having just gotten back from a one week excursion to wherever it is girls her age go, Noelle was full of stories about some mystery 'man' and all of the fine restaurants he took her to.

"What are you talking about, 'man' Do you mean, 'thug' because Red Lobster is hardly FINE dining Noelle." Attempting to give her a dose of her own nosy medicine I pushed her for more detail on what her version of a 'man' looked like. Taking the bait, Noelle continued to brag and worship this 'man's' every move.

"He handled everything and even bought me outfits to wear EVERY night." Noelle smacked her gum and waived her hand around in the air showing off what appeared to be an engagement ring.

Prior to my incident with Calvin, I couldn't escape her need to show me "the ring."

"So, what does this 'thug,' I mean 'man' DO for a living, if you don't mind me asking?

That's a pretty expensive piece of jewelry to be buyin' someone he barely even knows, don't ya think?"

I pressed her for more answers like she had done to me during the early days of my courtship with Calvin. Back in the day, there was no place to hide from Noelle with her never-ending list of inappropriate questions.

To me, her motives were those of an over-eager trainee who was simply looking to befriend a manager who could award her brownie points down the road. Not wanting to get a bad name or be considered unfriendly, I played along until things with Calvin started going south because that wasn't anything anyone REALLY wanted to know about, especially an "innocent" girl like Noelle.

As anticipated, Noelle's answer to my question about what her new "man" did for a living was vague because it paled in comparison to the flashy gem on her finger. "Oh, he's some head of some team for some company somewhere. Why should it matter?" Not liking the heat, Noelle retreated to other willing listeners who were just fine letting her regale them with the more important details of her fantasy weekend.

Shifting over into my seat on the airplane, Calvin had since fallen asleep and was now sprawled out into my lap. Hands that I once thought were sophisticated and manly were now merely the hands of a thief.

Hands that were supposed to love me and guide me were now hands that had assaulted me and robbed me of myself.

Remembering that last week prior to our trip to Orlando, I recognized a bitterness that I had never seen before in myself. Like a toxic virus, Calvin's anger and rage weren't only taking a toll on me physically. Well-meaning friends were beginning to take note of some other "changes" they were seeing in me.

"We don't see you at Church anymore and you barely even notice us when I see you at the grocery store. What's going on with you anyway?" Beth was one of those friends who would hunt you down if she didn't hear from me within a week. Her visits to me at the restaurant were now a regular occasion as that was the only place she said she could really SEE me. Any of my friends seeing me outside of work without Calvin, was simply out of the question.

Once upon a time, my friends would witness Calvin watching me talk to my cousin Alan in front of the movie theater. My cousin, who was a tall and athletic 28 year-old young man, was having a hard time making ends meet. Needing some money for a movie with his son, neither of whom I had seen for years, I was more than willing to chip in.

HIS DIRTY HANDS

By this point in my relationship with Calvin, it made sense to limit introductions to the rest of my family, especially family members that might suffer from the lens of Calvin's laser judgment. Not wanting to hear yet another one of Calvin's rants about the un-employed filching off his wallet, I opted to say less about a cousin, a cousin I practically never saw, until that afternoon anyway.

Friends would recall a loud screeching of tires in a relatively quiet parking lot that Sunday morning. Not realizing that Calvin had me on surveillance, apparently because he had nothing better to do on his day off, I would fail in my attempts to convince him that this young man was indeed my cousin. It wasn't until some of the McDonalds employees on break witnessed what was going on, that they were finally able to pry Calvin off of an innocent man.

Alan, trying his best to settle Calvin down yelling, "Man, I swear! I'm just gettin' some money for a movie. She's my cousin! What's the deal!" In retrospect, I gave Alan a lot of credit for keeping what he could of his cool, while his son watched his dad get attacked by a mad man.

"What do you mean getting money for a movie? You mean you can't pay for it yourself?"

Calvin looked like a mirror image of the man I had met in my restaurant when confronting those wanna-be thugs. It seemed Calvin made the same judgment about any man that wasn't him. Only Calvin would escape his own radar. He was merciless as he ripped Alan apart in front of his son.

In a moment no one would soon forget, Calvin turned to Alan's son and said, "Don't grow up to be like your father. You hear me? Even his own cousin is embarrassed to know him. Can't pay for his own movie, damn!"

Rumors about the incident swirled among our friends as many would insist that I should leave him. For reasons I may never understand, I made the choice to believe a territorial man who was simply protecting his property. A few friends still hung on in an effort to be my only lifeline. Friends like Beth who pleaded with me at the restaurant during one of my breaks.

"You just aren't the same when you're around him Demetria and you're starting to not be the same when you're without him either! Don't you think that is a problem? I mean, don't you miss your friends?"

Beth did her best to drive a wedge between me and a man who was really no good for me. There aren't too many friends out there who would put themselves in between a friend and the Devil, but Beth gave it her best shot.

HIS DIRTY HANDS

On more than a few occasions, she would even go head to head with him when he started making it a habit to answer my phone.

Quickly, he became able to systematically put a stop to all communication with many of my friends but Beth was one of the few who persisted. Infuriated with her tenacity, Calvin threw all of the niceties that should have been in place, out the window.

Accusing Beth of being jealous that I had a boyfriend only made her more resolute in her efforts to save me. This wasn't Beth's first introduction to an abuser. She had a story of her own that would prepare her for situations like mine with Calvin. This was presuming I'd listen. In his now predictably manipulative fashion, Calvin made sure conversations with Beth happened well outside earshot so that the truth of what was said, or not said, would always be in question.

As a result, friendships I had maintained for years started falling by the wayside as Calvin gained the upper-hand on my life. Before Calvin, Church was my social life and a safe haven for me. Now, sitting on a plane bound for Orlando, I remembered rainy Thursdays in a McDonalds full of rowdy teenagers. It wasn't too long ago, that I had looked at Calvin as my ticket out of a mundane, suburban life. He would argue that Church on Sundays was a waste of his time and everyone else's.

"All of that Holy Crap is for people who don't have anything going for themselves and who want to go and hide." He would insist that anyone involved in the Church was not to be trusted.

Calvin's aptitude for making wild and extreme judgments seemed to have its foundation somewhere in his childhood and wasn't something he was ever willing to elaborate on. Instead, he was methodical and calculating in his ability to rip and tear apart The Bible as if it were a work of fiction. "Everything can be disproved Demetria. You can't take those people at face value. They NEED to believe that their 'settling' ways are approved by God so that they don't have to try anymore. Can't you see that?"

Had his timing been any different, I would have laughed in his face. Instead, I was hungering for a way out and looking for any ammunition I could use to make the sound of a more exciting life just a little more guilt free.

Calvin was happy to oblige with story after story of the Church taking advantage of its followers in ways I used to ignore when watching the news.

Somehow, when Calvin told these stories, he spoke with just a hint of credibility.

This hint of credibility would be the only time I would ever hear anything genuine in this man's voice.

Gazing down at a man I no longer recognized, I wondered if he had ever opened up to anyone about what happened to him and the Church. His mom would be of no help either as she seemed resigned to a son who wouldn't budge or open up to anybody. "Dear, Calvin's just Calvin. He don't tell nothin' to nobody. He's his own man. Let him be." His mom spoke with a foreboding I should have paid attention to.

Heeding her advice and letting her "Calvin be Calvin", only amounted to a brutal man no one could relate to. I wondered what would have happened had I stood up to him sooner. Would that have prevented all of this damage or would I not be sitting here on this plane today? Would I be buried ten feet under? What was this man capable of?... and, the most important question, "Why wasn't I more afraid?"

The plane ride seemed like an eternity as my mind tried to make sense of a man and his methods. I knew that I would have to be prepared for this less-than man's consequences in response to my breaking up with him and moving on with my life.

I wasn't going to pretend any longer that I deserved any of what this man had to dish-out. Thankful for the moments of silence on that plane, it became crystal clear that I would have to be the one to exhibit faith. It was at this moment I decided to let God do the work he intended to do by first getting out of HIS way.

"This starts now" I thought, gently moving Calvin's hands back to his seat. Startled and completely forgetting that he was on a plane and not in our bedroom, Calvin sputtered and shouted, "What you wakin' me up for?" Passengers all turned to see what was playing out as I nodded my head back and forth in embarrassment. Calvin was also embarrassed in a moment I promised myself I would remember. It dawned on me that his controlling ways wouldn't always work to his advantage. I made a mental note of what might help give me leverage later. I thought, "he can't control the things that surprise him."

Managing to regain composure, Calvin wasted no time getting back to the rules and procedures that defined him. Bringing his seat to an upright and locked position, he was in perfect timing with the stewardess who announced our landing in Orlando. Oddly, I felt less fearful and less irritated by the man who I, just moments ago, considered a monster.

Under the bright light of a hot Orlando sun, was a man just like any other man. Gone was the sparkle I thought I saw when he bulldozed his way into my life. It's all how you market human behavior though as once upon a time, I considered him a prince.

Making our way down the aisle and onto the shuttle, I felt someone else's eyes on me. Unlike the distracting attention I would receive from a man who was waiting for me to get it wrong, these new eyes were those of God's as he encouraged me to press on.

"Where was this encouragement a year ago?" I muttered to myself, silently praying to have the courage and strength to keep my focus on an exit instead of just enduring a now spoiled and rotten relationship.

Calvin got to work barking orders at the driver making sure the driver knew that his luggage contained "valuables,"

While loading the luggage onto the shuttle the driver fell short of Calvin's expectations to everyone's delight. Vacationers love a good show and a fuming, Calvin was happy for the spotlight. Fuming, he grabbed his bag out of the driver's hands and methodically placed his on top of another piece of luggage marked "fragile."

Watching the scene with the shuttle driver play out for the world to see, Calvin seemed perfectly comfortable within the chaos he seemed to manufacture everywhere he went. Watching him grimace and berate this poor minimum-wage shuttle driver, he looked to his audience for some applause. "Really?" I thought. The "man" who once had me shaking to the bone with intimidation at a fancy steakhouse restaurant was literally an all-out buffoon.

Most of the poor bystanders on the shuttle were choking back laughs at a man who thought he was, "owning," it. With my head deeply burrowed in my lap, I cursed myself for not having insisted on going on vacation with him sooner. Perhaps I would have seen the REAL Calvin sooner.

Making his way to the seat beside me, he leaned over and took my hand like a man desperate for a life preserver. Not willing to help him out, I pulled my hand away muttering, "You should be ashamed of yourself." Calvin was caught off guard by my newfound confidence but too embarrassed to let it show. Our now captive audience in the shuttle continued to poke at the hornet's nest. One woman behind us let out a, "That's right! No one should be rewarded for that kinda behavior."

"Mind your OWN business" Calvin responded in his own defense. Grabbing my hand back, he attempted to regain the control he thought he had to begin with. No one was going to humiliate him in public like that, especially HIS woman. A younger man, who looked like he just stepped out of the gym, was sitting in the row beside us and saw Calvin exerting his will.

Standing up from his seat, this young man had to be 6'2 plus as he hulked over Calvin with a menacing grimace that could have been torn straight-out of a comic book. "Mam, do you need any help over here?" Bending down within eyeshot of Calvin, he continued, "Sir, why don't you give this kind lady her hand back?"

"Why don't you mind your own fucking business?!" Releasing my hand and rocketing up from his seat, Calvin shoved the young man down the aisle of the shuttle to everyone's horror. The audience that had willingly participated in a comedy show, were now scrambling for cover as the young man toppled over feet and anything else that happened to be in the way.

"Who do you think you're messin' with boy?" Calvin kicked and stomped at the young man in an attempt to publicly shame anyone who would come to my defense.

In the blink of an eye, what started as Calvin's temper tantrum with the shuttle driver and shuttle patrons was now Calvin's brutal attempt at setting the record straight about me.

The lady who spoke out earlier shouted, "Have you lost your mind?" After regaining his balance and footing, the young man managed to get enough momentum to bulldoze Calvin toward the front of the shuttle as the driver pulled over to the side of a very busy downtown Orlando.

"Get OUT! Both of you!" the shuttle driver barked through his handheld microphone. Not knowing whether he was talking to me, or whether he was talking to Calvin and the young man who tried to save me. My question didn't need any answering as the young man raced for the door.

Calvin, grabbing his bags from the cart, turned around expecting me to be behind him. Struggling with whether I should go with him or whether I should remain on the shuttle, the calm confidence that was now my best friend encouraged me to remain in my seat.

"Hurry up, mister!" the shuttle driver, more than annoyed, impatiently sounded the door alarm in an attempt to get this maniac off of his shuttle. Not unlike the French fry buzzer that first day at my restaurant, Calvin seemed to disintegrate before my very eyes as pieces of an elaborate puzzle started coming together. I recognized the sounds that would contribute to Calvin's undoing.

Understanding the psychology of this "less-than" man used to be as impossible as cracking the Da Vinci code. But now, with my new and unwavering commitment to a higher power, everything seemed easier and more clear.

"C'mon! Get your shit! Can't you hear the man?" Calvin did what Calvin always did when it came to delivering orders and commands. He had grown accustomed to my obedience, but things had changed since this new awakening, an awakening that began on the floor of my kitchen that awful night and continued on a plane bound for Orlando. Now on a shuttle in front of a crowd of onlookers, I faced the choice I should have made a long time ago.

"Don't go" the woman behind me said in a voice that was as deliberate as the shuttle's door alarm. Chanting, "don't go," in rhythmic fashion, over and over again.

"Get your SHIT and c'mon!" Calvin barked at me while what appeared to be an angel kept muttering "don't go."

Noticing my hesitation and terror at having to choose between staying on the bus or leaving with this mad man, the shuttle driver took the choice out of my hands shouting,"Not HER, YOU! Or else, my next call is 911!"

A massive traffic jam that was collecting behind the shuttle, threatened to shut down an entire lane of the street while drivers honked and shouted out of unrolled windows. Shoppers and tourists slowed down in hopes to catch some drama they might be able to watch on the local news. Not wanting to be THAT story, the shuttle driver added, "Last chance!"

Motioning for his phone, the shuttle driver started talking into his hand-free headset, alerting his corporate headquarters of a "developing incident" and asked them if calling 911 was the appropriate measure for an unruly passenger who couldn't stay in his seat.

Not wanting to wait for the authorities to get involved, Calvin picked up what he could of the luggage shouting, "I'll see YOU at the rental car office D-E-M-E-T-R-I-A." Applause broke out among the captive audience on the shuttle while Calvin mumbled, "ungrateful bitch."

Knocking into the sides of the doorframe, this was clearly not a man who was concerned about his 'fragile' luggage.

A man who was once the man of my dreams, a man I had proudly named Mr. Smooth, was instead a clumsy and fumbling womanizer who's only priority was the protection of his own 'fragile' ego.

As the shuttle pulled out, the woman behind me placed a firm hand on my shoulder saying, "you done right, honey. You done right. You gotta teach men like that a lesson or else life's by their rules." The woman who appeared to be in her mid-thirties spoke with a wisdom well beyond her years. Thinking about my mom in that instant, I wondered if this thing called 'wisdom' was in large part a matter of perspective.

Had my mom witnessed what had transpired on the shuttle that day, would she have the same words of advice as this well-meaning woman sitting behind me? Or, perhaps my mom would have responded to Calvin differently than I had. Maybe she wouldn't have shamed him in public and maybe she would have found a way to neutralize the situation instead of igniting it.

Maybe I had done myself a disservice by keeping my mom protected from the truth of Calvin's brutal ways.

Had she known that this latest episode was one of many, maybe this nightmare would finally be over.

Saddling up into the now empty seat beside me, the outspoken woman continued with her helpful advice, asking me "Now, what is this I hear about you meeting him at the rental car office?" Not one to appreciate all of the attention and spotlight, I felt oddly comfortable with this stranger as she asked questions that I would need to be prepared to answer by the time we reached our next stop.

"This isn't the first time is it?" she inquired. The long pause that followed answered her question. "I can see behind those big sunglasses sweetheart and it's a face I can unfortunately recognize." She went on to explain her own story of abuse with an ending that made me shiver to the core. Her sister had died at the hands of a man who behaved a whole lot like Calvin.

"You see, she didn't see the warning signs like I did. She didn't see that when his rage went public, that meant he'd get a whole lot worse in private." she pretended to be shuffling through her purse as tears fell down into shiny little pools on her lap.

"Nobody could warn her. Nobody could warn her!" she sobbed. Her shoulders slumped and heaving, I put my arm around her in an attempt to provide her with some amount of comfort. In between sobs and gasps she continued, "It is a darkness you will never know, a darkness your loved ones should never know! Goin' and meeting THAT man at the rental car office is a BAD idea. A bad, BAD idea."

Something genuine and piercing made it through my heart that afternoon. This feeling wasn't like any other I had let myself feel until now. I had to start reading the warning signs or be willing to suffer the consequences.

The consequences had already become too steep and now, in light of this well-meaning woman's story, I would be a fool not to take matters into my own hands. I would be damned to let a less-than man like Calvin take me away from my kids and family.

In the hurried moments between stops, this well-meaning stranger managed to give me counsel I let myself listen to. She introduced herself as Nancy, an Orlando native and mother of four children under the age of 16.

After the death of her sister, she had made it her mission to help other at-risk women get out of abusive relationships before it was too late.

She helped me devise a plan for my final exit out of Calvin's life. The first step would be to get a statement from the shuttle driver, providing me with valuable proof I could use later should I ever need it. Luckily the driver had already made a mental note of the man who was the instigator earlier in the trip and was more than happy to write a brief but punishing citation that I could issue as evidence to the police of his abusive treatment of me.

The plan would be to gather as much information as I could in order to expose Calvin for the batterer he was without risking my personal safety. Not getting off at the rental car company stop, I accepted Nancy's offer to drive me straight to the hotel.

Avoiding any additional scenes and securing a safe place to stay was the first order of business. Getting to the hotel before Calvin was all but guaranteed. I envisioned a very long line and yet another one of his tirades when he figured out that I had rented an economy and not luxury class car for our stay. To top it all off, he would be left waiting and waiting for an absent me as I would never show up while making my final exit.

Sitting in Nancy's Ford Mustang convertible as we raced down Interstate I-4, my mind raced at the thought of my new-found freedom.

"This is hardly a car for a woman with 4 children Nancy!" I laughed like a hyena for the first time in what felt like eons. "It didn't start out as mine! she responded. She seemed used to the question and went on to recite the story of an ex-boyfriend who couldn't afford the payments for a car he insisted SHE buy.

"Yeah, it took me a long time to realize the car was mine all along!" She informed me of a guy who almost convinced her to refinance her house in his name.

Eerily similar to Calvin's attempt to hijack my house, I thanked my lucky stars for this most unpredictable coincidence and sunk deep into the bucket seat of her car.

With eyes closed and wind whipping through my hair, I strategized what I would say to my mother once I got in the room. Nancy rattled on about her other 'mommy' car, a mini-van she used while shuttling the kids. This self-made woman reminded me of a me I had lost somewhere along the way.

In what seemed like the blink of an eye we were in the hotel lobby checking in. Nancy insisted she accompany me inside, just in case there were any problems.

After an effortless check-in, I assured her that I was just fine.

"You sure?" she asked, "Cause I can come up with you if you need some company and besides, I can help with the ex should he come around." Not wanting to put this poor any more out of her way, I re-assured her that I was fine and promised my attendance at brunch in the morning.

"I've got your room number now so if I don't see you at 9am, I know where to find you!" she warned as she laughed and skipped out the front doors and into her car. I admired the lightheartedness of my new friend and proceeded to the elevator with my bags. "I am going to be her again" I promised myself on the long ascent to the fourth floor of the hotel.

Hardly a hotel I would have picked, the halls screamed tacky. Flamingo pink wallpaper competed with lime green carpeting that glowed in the bright fluorescent lights of a hotel that wasn't hiding the fact it was trying too hard. The over-sized gold lacquered framed mirrors made it impossible to relax as I caught glimpses of myself at almost every angle.

Walking down the hotel's endless maze of halls, I remembered the fight that ensued when Calvin expressed his wish to stay here. The place seemed to be Spring Break central and not the luxurious hotel I had been promised for my "trip of a lifetime."

I could hear rowdy teens through the walls. The sounds of sex and the air of the unfaithful permeated every ounce of this place.

I gagged, choking back a cough as I walked past the cleaning crew working on a neighboring room. Apparently, the smell of the cheap, highly toxic cleaning products couldn't hide the indecency that happened in that room.

I wondered if it was too late to cancel the reservation and stay somewhere else. "That way, it will be impossible for him to find me" I thought. I could only imagine a desperate and infuriated Calvin combing the halls and knocking on doors to find me.

Finally making it to my room, a wave of relief washed over me as I was finally alone. Away from all of the public humiliation and away from the harsh lens of criticism, I leapt onto the king sized bed and started jumping on it like a child jumping on a trampoline for the very first time.

"Yes!" I jumped and jumped again, "YES!" After relishing a moment I wouldn't have shared with anybody, I remembered the extra-large soaking tub that seemed to be the hotel's only redeeming quality.

The brochure displayed images that looked like they were ripped right out of a Harlequin Romance novel. Perfectly manicured romantic couples cradled each other in a tub full of bubbles and rose petals. Being cradled by Calvin in a tub full of rose petals was the last thing in the world I could imagine after his series of assaults on me both physically and emotionally.

Now, with the place to myself, this tub was sure to be far more my style. Peeling off my tired traveling clothes, I made my way to the only dimly lit part of the room. Hearing the couple on the other side of the wall, I recognized the tell-tale signs of a domestic violence scene in progress.

A boyfriend or husband's open-ended questions followed by whimpers and sobs were followed by complete silence as the female victim would eventually learn how to submit. The all too familiar scene prompted me to turn the bathroom fan on with a commitment to call the hotel's front desk, if things got any more violent.

Distracted by the sounds coming from the other room, I fumbled with the knob to the sink's faucet in hopes for even more noise to drown out a reality I wanted so desperately to put behind me.

HIS DIRTY HANDS

It's funny how one's own personal experience adds a certain desperation and context to situations we once thought were normal or harmless.

The cries of a woman who could have been me, were louder and more urgent because I could relate to her experience. In the same way a newborn baby's cries are louder to its parents, this victim struck a similar chord in me.

Needing to put more light on the situation, I reached for the switch on the adjoining wall just as familiar hands reached around my neck, placing me in a strangle-hold I wasn't able to get out of. The scent of Calvin's high-end cologne included the industrial plastic aroma of the duct-tape he used to secure my hands.

My mouth now taped shut and unable to defend myself, Calvin dragged me out of the bathroom and onto the hotel room floor.

"Surprise D-E-M-E-T-R-I-A! Not the perfect way to start your trip of a lifetime now is it?" He wasn't able to duct tape my feet together due to the small confines of the hotel bathroom. The resulting sounds of my feet stomping and thudding must have blended with the noise next door because it seemed no one was coming to my rescue.

"You must be wondering how I was able to make it into OUR room and just how I was able to get here before you..." Wrapping my ankles in the duct-tape, Calvin sat perched on my lower back while I screamed and grunted to no avail.

"Seems you haven't learned any lessons yet, have you? You think your 'holier- than thou' ways are gonna get you outta this?" He chuckled in the sinister way reserved for bad-guys in the movies. In Calvin's case, it was no act.

"You think that it's OKAY to embarrass me like that in public, don't ya? You think that just because you pushed me to get a little outta hand that night, that you can cry to your momma. You think she'll just kick me to the curb, don't ya?" Pressing his weight into my lower back, Calvin got to his feet and started pacing the room like a caged animal.

Not able to turn over or get up on my feet, I was powerless on the floor as Calvin explained the $100 tip he gave to the front-desk so that he could "surprise" me by getting to Orlando early while on a business trip.

Apparently Calvin had stayed in this hotel before. The entire staff considered him VIP and treated him accordingly. It was the place he took all of his trainees.

Women who he thought were up to his rules and expectations were taken on the "trip of a lifetime."

After circling the room for what seemed like hours, he finally made his way back to the bed. Placing his foot on my neck, he gently pressed me further into the carpet. "YOU, have not passed the test D-E-M-E-T-R-I-A and have done some damage I won't be able to correct."

Frantically I squirmed, trying to get out from underneath his foot. I was losing precious air and wondered if there was any prayer I could say or promise I could make to the Lord above that would change the outcome of this nightmare.

Killing me quickly wasn't Calvin's style though. More like a cat who prefers torturing and playing with his prey, Calvin turned on the television and pumped up the volume so that my screams would be muffled by "Sin City," a movie that seemed perfectly timed for this occasion, in this disgustingly raunchy hotel, with this impossibly ego-centric less-than-man.

The bright lights of this hotel couldn't hide its darkness just like Calvin's glossy exterior couldn't hide the unrest living right underneath the surface. Kicking at my ribs and head, he would take his time preaching to me in a room that he considered HIS territory.

"You see, this is MY room and MY hotel. You didn't consider that did ya, when you were coming up with your little getaway strategy?" Wishing he would have duct-taped my ears shut, I did what I could to shield myself from his blows. Pretending to pass out only brought out the worst of what he had to deliver. "Don't go fallin' asleep on me cause' that just isn't any FUN... aren't we supposed to be having FUN?"

Grabbing me by the back of my hair, I recalled the incident on the kitchen floor. He had refrained from doing permanent damage then, but I wondered what he was capable of doing to me now. The thought of him not caring about committing permanent damage to me in a city with no witnesses, horrified me to new and deeper depths than I had ever thought possible.

"I will tell ya one thing, all this 'FUN' is gettin' me thirsty. Think I'm gonna get me a drink."

Calvin slowly sauntered toward the single closet in the room, opening it and pulling out one of his bags.

Inside, I beat myself up for not having been more suspicious. Why had I not considered he would be there waiting for me? Had I just unpacked and opened the closet, I could have done something, ANYTHING to protect myself.

Instead, I let my ego and trusting nature get the better of me. Watching him pull out a bottle of Jose' Cuervo, he slowly unwrapped one of the pre-packaged cups and reached into a nearly full ice bucket.

"You weren't payin' attention now were you D-E-M-E-T-R-I-A? You were just too busy jumpin' up and down on that bed like a maniac. Too busy not payin' attention to your man and thinkin' you had successfully left him at the rental car office."

He poured the cup full of tequila and started to drink it slowly. Too sore from his kicks and punches, I hoped this wouldn't last too much longer. Even if it meant that he killed me, I was resigned to what he had in store. Clearly, he had the upper-hand in a game he knew better than me.

I watched him take out his laptop and arrange it carefully on the bed. It shouldn't have surprised me that his wireless connection fired right on up as he navigated the internet with ease and landed on a porn site he had visited many, many times. It was a site I recognized as one of the sites he insisted on watching while with me.

"Now, I have another surprise I've been wantin' to share with you. A surprise I wasn't so sure I'd ever be able to share.

But now in light of your mistreatment of me, it's sure to be one you'll treasure."

Leaning down and hoisting me up and onto the bed. My body was faced down and my head crammed up on a pillow so I could see what he could see. Pulling my pants down he pressed play, forcing himself inside of me as we watched a video of Calvin having sex with a very willing Noelle on the very bed I was now held hostage on.

Trying to keep myself from vomiting, I tried to block the grunting sounds coming from above me and the all too familiar sounds of an over-excited Noelle in the background. Thrusting in and out with furious recklessness, he berated me, "You've done this to yourself D-E-M-E-T-R-I-A. You just couldn't play by the rules, could you? Look at her... isn't she beautiful? Now THIS is a girl who knows how to play by the rules."

In those darkest moments I wondered how many times Calvin had raped me. How many times was I actually willing to have sex with this man? Watching this Noelle, this tramp of a girl who others would claim didn't know any better had gotten the best of me.

Through the pounding of my head and brutality of his assault I could barely hear the knocking at the door.

Shocked that anyone would dare knock on the door while a sexual act that was so obviously in progress, Calvin barked, "Can't you see that we're busy in here! Unless you wanna participate, best you be gettin' gone!"

The knocking continued despite Calvin's threat.

"Demetria! You okay in there?" Over the blaring television and video, I could hear a now frantic Nancy twisting and turning the door handle.

"Honey, I can't hear you in there! Please do something to tell me that you're okay!" Knocking harder and louder, Calvin leapt to his feet and yelled, "She's fine whoever you are. She's in here with her husband. Mind your own business and be on your way, do you hear me!"

Nancy was relentless, "I'm not goin' anywhere until she speaks for herself!" This miracle, this angel had come to my rescue. There was no way he could get away with this now, not with Nancy threatening to break down the door.

Getting his pants on and grabbing the laptop, Calvin gathered his bags and rushed for the door. "You're not going to get away with this Demetria, you are going to pay one way or another."

It took only seconds for him to barrel through Nancy and race down the hotel hallway, down the stairs, and out the lobby doors. Because he always paid with cash, the hotel would have no real record of a Calvin Johnson. He was just as much of a mystery to them as he was to me. His charming ways had everyone fooled and his fits of rage kept everyone just a little too afraid to ask questions.

Upon finding me half naked and bound with duct-tape, Nancy, someone who just hours ago was a stranger, was now my saving grace. Our first call was to the Orlando police department and then a call to my mother's.

HIS DIRTY HANDS

SHOW FAITH... GET OUT

Calvin had not counted on my getting away. It seemed the plan was to kill me no matter what had happened on that shuttle.

My instinct to pull my hand away from him and not reward him for his public tantrum on the shuttle was the instinct that saved my life. Had I not instigated more of his rage that day, Nancy wouldn't have entered my life, she wouldn't have insisted on driving me to the hotel and walking into the hotel where she would hear my room number.

I would find out later that I had left my cell phone in Nancy's car and that she was simply coming back to my room to return it. Her instincts told her not to just leave it at the front desk.

Had it not been for that instinct, I wouldn't be sitting here today in this Church with my God and with a "ME" I can be proud of.

Calvin had come to Orlando with all of the tools necessary to end my life. I came to Orlando with a new-found faith in God and a promise to honor the path he laid out for me no matter how hard it would become.

I would come to find out that Calvin had no record of his existence anywhere. In the months that followed my horrendous trip to Orlando, I would have to come to terms with the danger I had put my entire family in by trusting blindly. Nights like those rainy Thursday nights seemed like heaven in comparison to the torture chamber that was my relationship with Calvin.

While it would be easy to place all of the blame on this monster, it became necessary for me to shoulder some of the responsibility. I manifested an exit to a life I should have been grateful for and should have been prepared to suffer the consequences.

I no longer beat myself up for not heeding Calvin's multiple warning signs because they now serve as lessons I can use in my mission to save more lives.

Domestic violence isn't just a buzzword or a faceless feel-good cause. Domestic violence is as real as the woman in the hotel room next door. She is as real as Nancy's sister who wouldn't listen to anyone because her pride was too big and self-confidence too drained to do anything about it.

Domestic violence isn't committed by just one gender. Domestic violence is the result of ego's that are left to run rampant in a society unwilling to do much about it. Domestic violence victims get tired of fighting back. It starts with the little things like how to load and unload a dishwasher or how to fold t-shirts. These little things may be little to us, but they mean the world to the offenders. These offenders feel that love and respect for THEM should be paramount to anything else.

Most domestic violence offenders feel let down by God, by their families or friends and will blame everyone else in an attempt to distract us from their own shortcomings. Well-meaning people allow themselves to get taken advantage of by offenders who oftentimes give the appearance of being put together, successful, and engaging.

Acting like chameleons, offenders will infiltrate every part of a victim's life, dismantling self-confidence and undermining a victim's ability to make decisions for themselves.

Domestic violence is a condition that endures as long as humans are humans. Nancy wasn't too unlike my friend Beth but there was one clear and concise difference.

Timing. It wasn't until I had made the commitment to my higher power, that I was even able to listen to those in my life who knew I deserved better. I had to know I deserved better before anything in my life was going to change. In order for that to happen, I had to exhibit FAITH. A lot of people will tell you they have faith but in my book, faith is a verb and something you do, not something you just "have."

Domestic Violence offenders are often victims too. I will never know the details of what happened to a Calvin who seemed so angry and disenfranchised. Someone, somewhere let him down in a very big way. Some will argue that evil doesn't need a reason or a root. My faith tells me otherwise. My faith tells me that Calvin was so busy controlling everything in his life, he never gave his faith a chance to operate.

I mistakenly thought that if I followed his rules, he would feel more relaxed and at ease in my love. I failed to recognize that feeling more relaxed and at ease in my love was something he never could have trusted. His real goal was to inflate and maintain his own ego through tests and games only he could win.

When I started asking questions and exposing him and his weaknesses, that is when I was in the most danger.

Not every story has a happy ending as the statistics of domestic violence related deaths have been on the incline since I was born. I wrote about my experiences in an effort to relate to some of you out there who think your lives are really under control.

HIS DIRTY HANDS

SHOW FAITH... GET OUT

If you fear your loved one's reaction to how you unload the groceries, unload the groceries, fold t-shirts... show faith, get out.

If your loved one accuses you of cheating all of the time and insists on answering and going through your phone, show faith... get out.

If your loved one hits you anywhere out of anger, show faith... get out.

If your loved one has to have it their way all of the time, show faith...get out.

If your loved one uses your friends or family against you and you feel there is nowhere to turn... show faith...get out.

It is my hope that you will share my story
with a loved one or friend
who might be in need of a lifeline.

God Bless,

NICOLE MERRITT

www.ingramcontent.com/pod-product-compliance
Lightning Source LLC
Chambersburg PA
CBHW060039040426
42331CB00032B/1407